LET'S PARLIAMO GLASGOW AGAIN

LET'S PARLIAMO GLASGOW AGAIN

Merrorapattur

Stanley Baxter

with

Alex Mitchell

Paul Harris Publishing

Edinburgh

First published 1983 by
Paul Harris Publishing
40 York Place
Edinburgh

Photographs of Mother Goose pantomime by Dennis Straughan
courtesy Edinburgh District Council, King's Theatre, © copyright
Edinburgh District Council, Department of Recreation
Photograph of 'Parliamo Glasgow' courtesy D C Thomson & Co Ltd
Photograph of Rosemary 'Helping the Bride' courtesy London
Weekend Television
Photograph of Stanley Baxter back cover and preface courtesy the
Evening Times, Glasgow

ISBN 0 86228 073 7

Typeset in Scotland by John G Eccles Printers Ltd., Inverness, and
printed by William Collins, Glasgow

CONTENTS

Illustrated with photographs of Stanley Baxter and the cast of "Mother Goose" in pantomime 1982-83 in Edinburgh and Glasgow.

Preface

It was, of course, pure coincidence that in the wake of the publication of the first Parliamo Glasgow book Professor John Honey of Leicester Polytechnic should allege, in a pamphlet, that Scots do not speak in an intelligible way.

When he went on to call for the abolition of that most distinctive and picturesque of languages, the Glasgow dialect, he gave my fellow-student, Alex Mitchell, and me a stunning shock.

Then, horror upon horror, we learned that Professor Honey advocates that we Scots should express ourselves in "educated Edinburgh or Kelvinside accents". Not only that. He declares that "The best thing a Scot can do is to come to England".

Not to put too fine a point on it, these outrageous statements ferr scunner't us, gi'ed us ra boak and had us ferr bilin'.

But, undaunted by the Sassenach professor's dreadful animadversions anent our lovely native tongue, I have pursued with unabated enthusiasm my research into Glaswegianology. And so I offer a second series of Parliamo Glasgow lessons.

For those who may want to know something of "educated Edinburgh and Kelvinside accents" I have ventured to add some pieces featuring Rosemary, a suburban lady, and Mr Ballhead, a gentleman whose speech patterns might not meet with the approval of Professor Honey.

Stanley Baxter

Parliamo Glasgow

Language of Romance

LECTURER:	Romance, of course, plays an important part in the lives of the young Glaswegian natives and it has its own distinctive and delightful phraseology. This is illustrated in a short scene from my latest play "The Flowering of Love", or to give it its Scottish title, "Bagzapaohin". We see two of the characters, Jimmy and his wife Nell, at a social function in the course of which they survey a young lady and gentleman who are enthusiastically demonstrating their high regard for one another.
JIMMY:	Look at ra baith o' rem! Snoggin' in front o' the hale cump'ny!
NELL:	S'awri', ra baith o rem's winchin'.
JIMMY:	Ra baith o' rem's aff thur chumps . . . Oh fur Goad's sake, they're still at it. It wid gie ye ra boak!
NELL:	Stoap lukkin' at them then.
JIMMY:	Ach let's beat it an' go fur a hauf.

LECTURER: Now it is patently obvious that Jimmy, a sensitive gentleman, does not approve of the uninhibited conduct of the damsel and her lover or, as he terms them,
RABAITHOREM
The wife Nell takes a laissez-faire attitude and points out that the young couple have formed a romantic liaison, or, as she puts it . . .
RABAITHOREMZWINCHIN
Jimmy is not at all impressed by this disclosure and employs the word —
ZAFFRUR
incorporating it in the sinister sentence
. . .
RABAITHOREMZAFFRURCHUMPS
Thus he indicates that, in his opinion, the demonstrative lovers are lacking in mental stability.
ZAFFRUR
is also used when speaking of an incorrigible person, or heidcase. Of him it may be said that he is . . .
ZAFFRURRAILS
On the other hand a lady will speak of her teetotal husband with approbation as she reveals that he is . . .
ZAFFRURUM
But back to our play. As the young persons plight their troth with continuous osculation they cause Jimmy

to give vent to a religious proclamation
. . .

OFURGOADSAKE!

Note the prefix . . .

OFUR

The addition of a single letter can change its meaning entirely. Like Jimmy, a gentleman urging his wife to accompany him to a hostelry for some refreshment will use the word . . .

GOFUR

as he suggests that they . . .

GOFUR AHOFURTU

As often as not his spouse will be quick to reply that she is . . .

NOFUR AHOFURTU.

Should her husband attempt to borrow money from her for the purchase of refreshments she is likely to make use of the following derivatives . . .

DOFUR, GOFUR, HOFUR, SOFUR and LOFUR

To these she adds certain other words to make her meaning absolutely clear. So she intimates to him that she has no cash for alcoholic beverages and requests him to forget his financial proposition . . .

AVNO DOFUR TAE GOFUR A HOFURTU, SOFUR GERRITYA LOFUR.

The wife will also be annoyed if her

young son uses the forbidden word
. . .

POFUR

as in his innocent question . . .

WHITSA POFUR?

But I digress. You may remember that our character Jimmy gave utterance to the lovely old word . . .

GIEYIRA

It occurred in his statement that the over-amorous machinations of the young lovers would induce a feeling of nausea in all who witnessed them. He declared that they would . . .

GIEYIRA BOAK.

GIEYIRA

is not infrequently heard in certain social circles and even on the football field. When one individual seeks to incapacitate another he will issue the warning . . .

AL GIEYIRA HEID

Later in the play the loving young couple adjourn to a discotheque. There the youthful Lothario discovers that the sum of £2 in the new coinage has vanished through a hole in his trouser pocket. His cry of dismay rings out . . .

GOARAVWENT IN LOAST-TWOPOUNBITS!

A short-sighted lady who finds herself by mistake in a masculine stronghold will also give voice to . . .

GOARAVWENTIN

Her discomfiture at her social gaffe will be expressed in the agonised cry . . .

GOARAVWENTIN TAERAGENTS!

An equally disconcerting mishap attends the maiden in our play. While dancing energetically in the discotheque she stops suddenly and renders the haunting lament . . .

GOARAVWENTIN

SPLITRASEAMS

OMAJEANS

Soon she delivers herself of an even more tragic verse. It begins with the heart-rending cry . . .

RERSIZ

followed by. . .

OOTMABLIDDISLAX

And so the full extent of the calamity is conveyed in the touching refrain . . .

RERSIZ OOTMABLIDDISLAX!

The Professor on a

Shopping Expedition

I was more than delighted when, quite by chance, I found myself in the establishment of a small trader and made some valuable discoveries concerning the enchanting patois spoken by the natives of the great city on the Clyde.

I had been invited to a small gathering in the home of a resident in the impressive boulevard known as *RAGALLAGATE*. Custom decreed that I should take with me what is termed *ALITRORAMAMMIMINE*. So there I was in the modest premises, or *BEERSHOPE*, in search of a bottle of wine.

The establishment was crowded with ladies and gentlemen purchasing various beverages for their delectation at the week-end. No sooner had I entered when I found myself in close proximity to a stout matron. Judge of my perturbation when she turned to me and made the grave allegation that I was guilty of moral turpitude. Looking at me intently, she cried . . . *"HOOR!"*

Then suddenly to my great relief she revealed that she was indulging in a guessing game. She put the question . . . *"HOORYESHUVVIN?"* I had to confess that I was quite ignorant of her identity. She herself enlightened me and told that her name was *LENA FAMMUHURDIZ*. I responded at once with a hearty "How do you do, Madam Fammuhurdiz?" Alas, the lady had quickly lost interest in the guessing game. She turned to the damsel behind the counter and complained about the delay in being served. To my astonishment the ensuing conversation was conducted in what I had no doubt was the language of ancient Rome. The large lady observed . . . *"AMGERRINRATTI"*. From the serving maiden came the reply . . . *"AVONLI WANPERRAHONS"*.

The conversation was terminated by Madam Fammuhurdiz taking her leave of the shoplass with the expressive Gaelic phrase *"STUFFYOONYURROATTONSHOPE!"* As she hastened from the beershope the large lady bade me farewell with the not dissimilar word, *"STUFFYOONAWYAMUG!"*

Soon the damsel behind the counter was devoting her attention to a housewife and her small daughter who, it appeared bore the name "Hannah". The housewife addressed the serving maiden as "Anna". The linguistic prowess of the Glaswegian native was strikingly demonstrated when the young mother spoke in Japanese. Vivaciously she hailed the shoplass with *"HAWANNA!"* Next she made her wants known with *"AWANNABANANAFURMAHANNAH"*. From across the counter came the reply in the authentic argot of Tokyo — *"YIJISWAANTRA WANBANANAHANNA?"* The banana was handed over and the housewife indicated that she wished to purchase a pan loaf . . . *"ANAWANNAPANANNA"*.

Then she remembered a request made to her by her

husband, Dan, a lover of football. Dan had directed her to bring him a can of liquid sustenance. She pointed to the can and again came the accents of the Far East . . . "GEISHA", she began, *"GEISHACANFURMAMAN-DANRAFAN"*.

But the young matron had not yet completed her shopping. She espied on a high shelf a small bowl which she decided to acquire for her pet bird's cage. The damsel behind the counter then disclosed that she had no head for heights and declined to climb up the step-ladder to procure the small bowl. She demurred with the word . . . *"ADTUMMULAFF"*. The customer made the comment, *"WUDJI?"* and volunteered to hold the step-ladder steady. She gave the undertaking, *"ALHUDJI ALNONUDJI"*.

Still the damsel refused to mount the steps and bring down the bowl for the bird's cage. The housewife, her heart set on purchasing the bowl, issued the stern command, *"WUDJI GERRATBOUL!"*

The rely was an emphatic negative. At this juncture, I regret to say, the young housewife became extremely exasperated. But, despite her ire, she demonstrated the Glaswegian native's innate love of poetry in the lyrical rebuke she directed at the obstinate maiden who refused to provide her with the pet bird's bowl . . . I listened entranced as she declaimed —

AHYADUDJI AHCANNIBUDJI
AHWANTITRATBOUL
FURMABUDJIZCLUDJI!

Parliamo Glasgow

Upatraburd's

LECTURER: We illustrate this language lesson with a playlet in which we hear the native patois as it is spoken in a Glaswegian home. First of all we see a mother and father seated in the kitchen of their residence. They are silent until the doorbell rings.

MOTHER: Ratsa door! Whit ur ye sittin' therr in yur simmit fur? Pirroan yur jaickit!

FATHER: Eh?

MOTHER: Yur jaickit! It'll be Ella an' hur fella!

FATHER: Aw, izzi aff his work?

MOTHER: He's took ra night aff.

THE FATHER STRUGGLES INTO HIS JACKET. THE MOTHER HURRIES TO OPEN THE FRONT DOOR. SHE RETURNS TO THE KITCHEN WITH HER DAUGHTER ELLA AND THE BOY FRIEND, SAMMY. THE YOUNG MAN IS CARRYING AN UMBRELLA.

FATHER:	Aw Ella's fella lumburs hur hame wi' a numburella!
SAMMY:	(RESENTFULLY) Why ra hell should Ella's fella no' lumbur Ella wi' a numburella?
ELLA:	Ach gi'es ra gamp. (SHE SNATCHES THE UMBRELLA AND THROWS IT INTO A CORNER. THEN SHE ADDRESSES HER PARENTS) Ur youse yins no' gaun' oot?
MOTHER:	Naw . . . Thur nae binga oan ra night.
SAMMY:	(ASIDE TO ELLA) Heh, you sayed if Ah came up here the night we'd be able tae . . .
ELLA:	Shurrit. (TO PARENTS) Ur yiz no' gaun' ben the hoose tae watch ra telly?
FATHER:	Naw . . . Ra telly's broke.
SAMMY:	(HANDING THE FATHER A BANK-NOTE) Away you wi' the wife an' huv a wee bevvy.
MOTHER:	Oh, 'sa fiver!
FATHER:	(TO SAMMY) Huv you stertit workin' overtime?
SAMMY:	Naw . . . No' till you an' yur missus leaves the hoose.
FATHER:	(TO MOTHER) Come oan, Cynthia. Doon tae ra pub.
	THE PARENTS EXIT.
	SAMMY IMMEDIATELY CLASPS ELLA TO HIM.
ELLA:	Lay aff, ya nyaff! Ma wee sister'll be here in a minnit!

SAMMY:	Yur wee sister nixt!! You sayed if Ah came up here the night we'd . . .
ELLA:	Cley up . . . Here she's noo.
	GIRL ENTERS. SHE IS ATTRAC- TIVE AND WEARING A VERY SHORT SKIRT. SAMMY GAPES AT HER.
SAMMY:	So THIS is yur sister?
SISTER:	That's right . . . Jist youse carry on. Ah'm gaun' tae ra disco . . . But Ah'm gaun' ben tae the room first. Thur's a cake in therr an' Ah'm dyin' fur a slice o' it.
	THE SISTER EXITS.
ELLA:	(COYLY) She's gaun oot! We'll huv the hoose tae wursel's!
	SHE PUTS HER ARMS ROUND SAMMY'S NECK.
	BUT HE DISENGAGES AND MAKES FOR THE DOOR.
ELLA:	Ur ye gaun 'tae ra loo?
SAMMY:	Naw, ben tae ra room fur a slice o' cake.
ELLA:	Ya waster! Gaun' take a rinnin' jump tae yursel'!

*   *   *   *

LECTURER:	Let us consider some of the more obscure words and phrases we have heard in the drama enacted in the home of the young lady, Ella. As the doorbell heralds the approach of the

21

lovers her mother reproaches her husband with three scornful words . . .

SITTIN ERRINYUR SIMMIT!

Clearly she is of the opinion that a simmit, or vest, is not the correct dress for one who is about to receive a guest in his home.

ERRINYUR

is freqently used by ladies when they are critical of their husband's sartorial deficiences. So we have such variations as . . .

STAUNNIN ERRINYUR SHURT!
LYIN ERRINYUR GUIDSUIT!
FLOATINABOOT ERRINYUR BERR-SPUDS!

And a fastidious matron who objects to her spouse's unconventional night attire might be heard to declaim . . .

SLEEPIN ERRINYUR COAMBIES!

The father in our play inquiries if his daughter's gentleman friend is taking the evening off from his employment. He asks . . .

IZZIAFFIZ WURK?

Note the word . . .

IZZIAFFIZ

We use it as a prefix when seeking information. If we are concerned about a male person's emaciated appearance we pose the question . . .

IZZIAFFIZ CHUCK?

Should we wish to determine whether or not he has ceased to indulge in the immoderate consumption of alcohol, we ask . . .

IZZIAFFIZ BOOZIN?

If we become aware that a gentleman's behavioural pattern is tending towards the unorthodox then we say . . .

IZZIAFFIZ RUDDIROACKUR?

More interesting words are heard when the lovers arrive at the house. The father derides his daughter's gentleman friend, or lumbur, for escorting her home with an umbrella. Spiritedly the gallant demands to know why he should not . . .

LUMBUR ELLA WIA NUMBURELLA

You will notice that the letter "n" is added to the final word. So it appears as . . .

NUMBURELLA

A word beginning with the letter "n" is often preceded by . . .

ZATNOA

A Glasgow native who treats with contumely a marital partner, politician or a television "personality" who rouses his or her ire is apt to exclaim . . .

ZATNOA NASSIAFULLA?

And, of course, from one who receives an inflated gas or electricity bill or income tax demand there comes the familiar cry of despair . . .

ZATNOA NOFFISEEKNUR?

Two other words denoting deep sorrow were spoken by the father and mother in the domestic drama. These were . . .

NAEBINGA-OANRANI' and *RATEL-LISBROKE*

Greatly heartened, they depart when the young man gives them the wherewithal to refresh themselves at a nearby hostelry. Their daughter Ella finds herself in the arms of her ardent wooer. He is not lacking in frankness as he makes the proposition . . .

WHIRRABOORRA BASHATRA-PASH?

The young lady appeals to him to moderate the intensity of his passion. She addresses him with the delightful rhyming word . . .

LAYAFF-YANYAFF

In similar circumstances she could have made an even more emphatic request by using another rhyming word . . .

CURRITOOT-YADURTIBROOT

or, in an even greater emergency . . .

NUFARATYARANDIRAT!

The lovers are again disturbed when the young sister appears on the scene. But she announces that she will adjourn to another apartment to partake of a slice of the cake she has purchased. Then she makes her tactful exit and Ella embraces the lumbur, Sammy. Suddenly he tears himself from her arms and makes for the door. Anxiously she inquires . . .

URYI GONTIRALOO?

She no doubt expected him to echo the word and reply . . .

AYAM GONTIRALOO, TOORA-LOORANOO

But he did not utter these lovely words. Instead he stated that he was going to join her young sister and request her to give him a slice of her cake. With fominine intultion the maiden Ella concludes that the young man's primary desire is not for a piece of cake. And so, from the disillusioned damsel, we hear the age-old cry that has ended not a few Glasgovian romances . . .

GONTAKKARINNINJUMP-TIYURSEL!

Parliamo Glasgow

Tips for Tourists

LECTURER:	There are times when French, German, English and other foreign visitors to Glasgow have difficulty in understanding and being understood by some of the natives with whom they come in contact.
	This lesson is designed to help our non-Glaswegian friends to overcome certain linguistic impasses that may present themselves.
	We commence with a sketch about a tourist from south of the border who is paying his first visit to the city.
	THE TOURIST IS IN A TAXI AND IS IN CONVERSATION WITH THE DRIVER.
TOURIST:	Drop me off at a decent restaurant.
DRIVER:	Ur ye furra tightnur?
TOURIST:	I want to have dinner.
DRIVER:	Hud ye heehaw tae eat oan the train?
TOURIST:	They were not serving heehaw or any other dish. There was no dining-car.

THE TAXI STOPS OUTSIDE A RES-
TAURANT

DRIVER: This is no' too bad a j'int.

TOURIST: (LEAVING THE TAXI) What do I owe you?

DRIVER: Three quid.

TOURIST: What? That's an exorbitant charge!

DRIVER: Rat's ra ferr.

THE TOURIST, SCOWLING, HANDS OVER THREE £1-NOTES AND STALKS OFF TOWARDS THE RES-TAURANT. THE DRIVER CALLS AF-TER HIM.

DRIVER: Heh, is thur heehaw tip?

THE TOURIST IGNORES HIM AND ENTERS THE RESTAURANT. AS HE TAKES HIS MEAL HE IS INTRIGUED BY THE CONVERSATION OF A YOUNG COUPLE AT A NEARBY TABLE.

GIRL: Chuck us ower a bap, pal . . . an' see's a glessa ra rid biddy.

MAN: Ah could dae wi' merr totties an' tum-shie.

GIRL: Ur you no' ferr stappit noo?

MAN: Shut yur gub an' drink yur vino.

MYSTIFIED BY THIS EXCHANGE, THE TOURIST FINISHES HIS DIN-NER AND CALLS FOR THE BILL. HE IS SHOCKED AT THE LARGE AMOUNT HE IS BEING CHARGED.

TOURIST: (TO WAITER) This is absolutely out-

	rageous! £10 for a small fish and a few chips and a glass of wine that tastes like vinegar!
WAITER:	Keep yur herr oan.
	THE TOURIST FLINGS A £5-NOTE ON THE TABLE AND WALKS OFF.
TOURIST:	You're getting heehaw tenner out of ME!

    *   *   *   *

LECTURER:	It is small wonder that the tourist in our sketch is nonplussed by some of the native expressions he hears. Let us try to determine the significance of these When he asks to be taken to a restaurant he is rather baffled by the taxi-driver's question . . .
	URYEFURRA TYTNUR?
	URYEFURRA
	is more frequently used with the affix . . .
	HOF
	This gives us the much-appreciated invitation . . .
	URYEFURRAHOF?
	A gentleman who has accepted too many such invitations may express his dread at being confronted by his wife. He will then be asked the grave question . . .
	URYEFURRAHIJUMP

We next come to another inquiry from the taxi-driver that puzzled his passenger. He asks if, on the train from London, he had . . .

HEEHAWTI EAT

Under the impression that the driver was referring to some sort of native dish, the tourist replies that no meal was served on the train, let alone . . .

HEEHAWTI

The tourist complains that the £3 fare for the one-mile journey is far too much. Nevertheless he hands over the money. The taxi-driver is disappointed at not receiving the expected gratuity. Again he uses the word . . .

HEEHAWTI

He adds a single letter to convey his resentment. And so the word changes to . . .

HEEHAWTIP!

Had the tourist been au fait with the Glasgow patois he could have censured the taxi-driver by exclaiming . . .

YURRATTITMAC!
CUMMAFFITYU!

or

TAKMEFURRAMUGPAL?

In the restaurant the tourist is at a loss to understand the purport of the conversational exchange between the young lady and her gentleman friend at an adjacent table. She makes known her desire for an additional bread roll with the enchanting adjuration . . .

CHUKKUZOURABAPAL

Next she expresses a wish for wine, using the traditional form of request . . .

SEEZAGLESSARARIDBIDDI

Her escort seems a little distrait. He is anxious to obtain a second serving of the ancient Scottish delicacy . . .

TOTTIZANTUMSHI

Suddenly the damsel realises that her dinner companion is proving to be too hearty a trencherman. Her concern on this score is demonstrated by her query . . .

URYUNO FERRSTAPPITNU?

The young gentleman ignores her warning. He invites her to perform the remarkable feat of imbibing wine with her mouth closed. He makes the suggestion . . .

SHUTYURGUB ANDRINKUPYUR-VINO

Meanwhile the tourist has finished his dinner and asks for his bill. He makes a violent protest at the amount he is being charged. The waiter deals with the situation by intoning . . .

KEEPYUR HERROAN

By this he means that the gentleman should preserve his equanimity.

KEEPYUR

is a key word in the Glasgois vocabulary. An appeal for calm is also effected in the advice . . .

KEEPYURHEID

or more pedantically . . .

RETAINRACRANIUM

The meaning of the word changes subtly when a lady counsels her young daughter about the pitfalls that may await her when she goes out into the world. The mother will then use . . .

KEEPYUR

with the addition of the word . . .

HONOANYURHAPNI

and so we have the stern maternal warning . . .

KEEPYUR HONOANYURHAPNI

As our sketch ends we see the infuriated tourist refusing to pay the £10 bill. As he throws a £5-note on the table and hurries from the restaurant he improvises on a native word he has learned and informs the waiter that he will receive . . .

HEEHAWTENNER!

The Professor has

One Enchanted Evening

Before commencing my sociological research in Glasgow and its environs I had been informed by a learned friend that to spend a Sunday evening in that jewel of a city was a unique experience that stamped itself indelibly upon the memory. "There is," declared my friend, "nothing like it in the rest of the world".

Accordingly I wasted no time in savouring the Sunday evening delights of the great metropolis.

What an ambience of gaiety prevailed as I joined the throng of merrymakers who paraded the pavements which sparkled under a deluge of soft West of Scotland rain. Not a few of the promenaders spoke in a foreign tongue.

One lady revealed that the influence of the old Franco-Scottish Alliance was still extant. After a particularly heavy shower of rain she drew her husband's attention to her wet outer garment. Speaking in French, she asked him . . .

DIEU SI MA CÔTÉ?

or, to give it its Glaswegian spelling . . .

DYESEEMACOATEH?

Her husband pointed out that his coat, too, was far

from dry. To my astonishment he elected to use the German language. He began his reply with . . .

ACH MEIN GOTT

Then he added a word in what I took to be the Bavarian vernacular . . .

BLIDDISOAKTHRÜ

So that his statement in full was . . .

ACH MEIN GOTT BLIDDISOAKTHRU

Happily most of the Sunday evening revellers preferred to converse in the lovely liquid accents of their native habitat. One youthful couple were partaking of an al fresco repast of fish and pommes frites. These they carried in paper bags. From the young lady came the observation . . .

SNOMUCHIA

to which she added the attractive words . . .

SUPPURFUR RAMUNNI

Her gentleman friend appeared to concur with her verdict on the meal and proclaimed . . .

SADAMPTSWINNUL!

Then impulsively he paid the damsel a graceful compliment, likening her to a Greek goddess . . .

YURDIALZAWGREECE

She in turn praised the beauty of his visage, telling him . . .

ALIKEYURBLOOMINCHEEK

And she bade him regard the reflection of his handsome countenance in a looking-glass with the charming suggestion . . .

TAKKADEKKATYUR AINDAMPAN

It was not long ere I realised that it was trysting-time for lovers. One young swain braved the downpour as he

awaited his lovely young inamorata. When she arrived she was hailed with a fervent cry of . . .
AH, LOVE!

But it seemed to me that there was a soupcon of irony in his tone when he appended the word . . .
GETTINDROONDIT
and his greeting took the form of . . .
ALLUV GETTINDROONDIT

But it was obvious to me that her cavalier, or lumbur, was prepared to overlook the late arrival of the damsel. What tenderness there was in his voice as he paid tribute to her with a quotation from a moving Gaelic love-poem . . .
AYEYURTHERR
SJISTNUTTFERR
MACLAEZIZSOAKIN
ANYIDONTGIADOACKIN

Overcome by emotion, the young lady then addressed her amour by his full and impressive cognomen, crying . . .
MONTY! MONTY!
MONTY HELLOOTAHERE!

It was something of a revelation to me when I observed that many of the natives were patrons of the cinema. As they approach a film theatre their custom is to stop suddenly and give vent to the ritual chant . . .
THURRACUE! THURRACUE! THURRACUE
AMILELONG!

I was saddened by the sight of one elderly gentleman who passed me. He, it would seem, nurtured a hopeless passion for a screen idol of yesteryear. There was nostalgia in his voice as he called her name . . .

AVA! OH, AVA!
and he went on to express his devotion to her in the old Gallowgatean dialect . . .
AVA! AVAHELLAVA THURSTOANMI!

As the jolly Sunday evening wore on, the happy throng, splashing merrily through the rain, was augmented by a strange and picturesque band of young natives, male and female. They wore shorts and bore on their backs heavy burdens from which hung pots, kettles, guitars and sundry other articles. I concluded that they were itinerant merchants from the remote trading post known as Rabarras.

I smiled upon one of the young females of the tribe and offered to purchase one of the antique cooking utensils suspended from her pack. To my delight she not only spoke English but intimated that she would make me a present of one of her wares. "I'll give you this pot," she told me.

Then, lapsing into the obscure argot of Rabarras, she continued . . .
ALGIEYIT OWERYUR BALDIOLCRUST

What a delightful end to an evening of enchantment!

Parliamo Glasgow

Broadcasting Techniques

LECTURER: I would like, if I may, to draw your attention to some of the words and phrases we hear, perhaps too frequently, from radio and television broadcasters. I trust that these ladies and gentlemen may draw some slight benefit from the theories I am about to propound.

It is a matter for regret that they rarely, if ever, make use of the beautiful language spoken by many of their Scottish listeners.

One of the oft-repeated sayings heard over the air is "Thank you very much indeed." This is directed at persons who have given interviews. Perhaps it could be replaced by such Glaswegian expressions of gratitude as . . .
THANXALOT
FERRANUFFMAC
or even
TAPAL

All too often in television plays a lady or gentleman will make an exit with the intimation, "I'll see myself out". I suggest that this might be changed, in Scottish plays at least, to . . .

AMFURRAFF

ALFINDRADOORMASEL

or the more specific

DONTGERRUP, CHEERIBYRANOO

In dramatic works emanating from the United States characters frequently pose the brusque question, "What are you talking about?" Desirable variants are . . .

WHISSATYUSAYED?

WHIDDYEMEAN?

WHITTURYEGERRINAT?

Greatly do I admire the solicitude shown to the victims of untoward occurrences in television dramas. A lady or gentleman knocked to the ground by a malefactor, hurled from a blazing motorcar, thrown from a high building or otherwise rendered hors de combat will, as often as not, find a person bending over them and inquiring anxiously, "Are you all right?"

I submit that it might be more true to life if they employed the traditional Glaswegian expressions of concern . . .

HOOHUTYI?

HOOGIEDYIRAKEEKUR?
JIWAANTA CUPLASPRIN?
or the even more compassionate
GETRASOWLABRANDY
You may have noticed that the players
in American television dramas are
peculiarly addicted to the pleasures of
the table. A gentleman will lure a pre-
possessing damsel into his company
by inviting her to accompany him to a
"li'l Mexican place downtown where
we kin gedda marvullus chili con
carne". Almost invariably the young
lady exclaims, "Yeah, Ah sure wud
like that." Were she a Glasgow
maiden she would be accustomed to a
much greater variety in the forms of
invitations to dine out. Such as . . .
MOANFURRACOAFFY
ALSTONYIA BAGGACHIPS
FANCIATYTNUR?
And the seal has been set on many a
romantic liaison with the tender query
. . .
COODJI GOAPIE?
One television expert who explains to
us the intricacies of football is wont to
proclaim, "That's a good-looking ball!"
He is not, of course, referring to the
agreeable rotundity of the leathern
sphere but to the accuracy with which
one player has propelled it to a col-

league on the field. I suggest that the expert might vary his encomium with such attractive Glaswegianisms as . . .

THASSARERRBAW!
RATPASSIZMAAAAAGIC!
IZPITTITAERAFITTOKENNY!

Let us consider now the weather forecasts. Interest in these would be heightened if they were couched in these vivid meteorological terms . . .

SGONNICUMDOON CATSANDUGZ
CERRIABROLLIRAMORRA
MERRSNAW, PIRROANYUR-
WELLIZ

and warning us of low temperatures in prospect . . .

KEEPOANYURCOAMBIZ

and

NORAWERRUR FURBRASS-
MUNGKIZ

I am most grateful to you for giving me your attention. Thank you very much indeed . . . er . . .

AWCHINAS THANXAMILLYUN.

The Professor
In the Park

What a treasure trove of linguistic gems I lighted upon when my study of Glaswegianology took me to one of the great city's public parks! I found it full of happy citizens, male and female of all ages. Soon I was taking copious notes of the beautiful words and phrases that fell from their lips.

But I must confess to some apprehension when I heard a matron menacing her small offspring with a peculiar form of chastisement. It appeared that he had reiterated a strong desire for ice-cream and she threatened him with . . .

ALPOKEYHATYE!

Then, to a lady who accompanied her, she made an astounding statement about her diminutive son. I translated it as meaning that he was a crimson sea bird. She declared . . .

RATWEANZA RUDDIGANNET

Next she put forward the incredible claim that he was aided in his consumption of ice cream by an orchestral accompaniment. She contended that he could eat it . . .

TIABAUNPLAYN

I waited in the hope of seeing the infant virtuoso

perform his masticatory feat. But his mother refused to purchase more ice-cream. She did, however, promise him what I imagined was a Scottish delicacy . . .

ASCUDOANRALUG

Leaving the happy family, I made my way into the rustic recesses of the park. There I encountered two maidens in swimming attire who were lying at their ease on the greensward. My curiosity was aroused when one of them, a comely redhead, revealed to a passing acquaintance that they were waiting for . . .

RASSUNTI

Was this, I asked myself, the name of a religious leader revered by the natives and about to pay them a pastoral visit? But I rejected this theory when the maiden called out . . .

KUMMOOT

After some concentration I came to the conclusion that the young ladies wished to acquire a tan and were waiting for . . .

RASSUNTI KUMMOOT

I was congratulating myself on determining the meaning of the phrase when I perceived two young gentlemen who were surveying with interest the recumbent females. One of the gallants remarked to his friend, Noah . . .

NOAH BADPERRABURDS

The other addressed his friend as "Ivan" . . .

IVAN EYEFURRARIDHEID

Eventually the two young ladies became aware of their admirers' presence. The badinage that ensued illustrated the remarkable linguistic versatility of the great city's inhabitants. The red-haired Glaswegienne called to the young males in Russian . . .

AWSKI DADDLE . . . BUGGRAFF!

Her admirer, Ivan, at once hailed her by her exotic Russian name . . .

GITNOATTITYA NASTIBITCH

As I am not versed in any of the Slavonic languages, I left the quartet to their exchange of pleasantries and bent my steps towards a large lake. Many Clydesiders, with their traditional love of maritime pursuits, were braving the watery element in small craft known as

OARIBOATS

It was heartening to see how assiduously the heads of families taught their progeny the intricacies of seamanship. One juvenile who proposed to take his parents on a voyage over the lake was not fully conversant with the technique of rowing. His father at once issued the nautical command . . .

YURERSS TAERASHERPEND!

Alas, the oarsman stood up to change his position on the seat and caused the craft to turn over. He and his parents were precipitated into the water and were obliged to wade ashore. Crestfallen over his error, the embryo mariner ran off. His father hurried after him, promising to give him further navigational instruction. In his distinctive patois he assured him . . .

ALLERNYI TICOWPRABOAAAT

As I made my way towards the park exit I passed the red-haired young lady and her companion. They now lay upon their backs in the sunshine. I ventured to address them in their own language with . . .

RASSUNZOOTNOO!

The red-haired damsel immediately sat upright and

regarded me with an interest I found quite flattering. All at once, in the lilting language of the Gael, she trilled . . .
ALPITMA
adding a word to it to complete what I had no doubt was an ancient Hebridean blessing . . .
ALPITMA FITUPYURJAXI!

Parliamo Glasgow

The IT People

LECTURER:	A language most non-Glaswegians find rather difficult to understand is that spoken by certain inhabitants who, in their discourse, feature the syllable "IT". We illustrate this in a playlet in which we see two of the IT people, Margrit and Dauvit, attending a charity bazaar.
DAUVIT:	Whit is it, Margrit?
MARGRIT:	'Sa jumble, Dauvit. Let's tak a dek at it.
DAUVIT:	Ah don't fancy it.
MARGRIT:	Aw, stoap moanin' aboot it! C'm oan inty it . . . Here a stall wi' claes fur sale oan it.
DAUVIT:	Ach Ah see it.
MARGRIT:	Erra rerr checkit jaickit oan it, Dauvit. Whit aboot it?
DAUVIT:	Whit aboot whit?
MARGRIT:	Aw, ye're real glaikit. Ra nice checkit jaickit! It's smart, intit?
DAUVIT:	Ah'd reyther go nakit than werr that dampt jaickit!

MARGRIT:	Try it. Pit it oan.
	DAUVIT GIVES IN AND PUTS ON THE JACKET.
DAUVIT:	It's not bad, intit no'?
MARGRIT:	Whit a rerr fit, Dauvit!
	THE WOMAN IN CHARGE OF THE STALL APPEARS
DAUVIT:	(TO WOMAN) Whidd'ye waant fur it?
WOMAN:	Waant fur whit?
DAUVIT:	This checkit jaickit.
WOMAN:	Aw, it? A fifty-pee bit an' ye can huv it.
	A BURLY MAN IN HIS SHIRT SLEEVES RUNS UP TO THE STALL AND ANGRILY ADDRESSES DAUVIT.
MAN:	Dammit, that's ma jaickit! Gi'e's it!
WOMAN:	Ah sell't it.
MAN:	You should get yur heid feltit.
MARGRIT:	Aff wi' it, Dauvit! Gi'e him it afore ye get beltit.

* * * *

LECTURER:	The regrettable contretemps at the clothing stall provides us with some typical speech patterns of the IT-speakers. The young man, Dauvit, is not sure about what is taking place in the hall. He queries his sweetheart with a word often used in the language . . .
	WHITIZZIT?

Other kindred words are . . .

WHERRIZZIT?

and the more obscure . . .

WHYRAHELLIZZIT?

which is used by a female of the IT tribe when she disapproves of her husband's inability to cope with a surfeit of liquid refreshments. To it she appends a second word, and so we have the pertinent question . . .

WHYRAHELLIZZIT YUTAKKIT-WHENYICANNIHODDIT?

In our playlet the young lady, Margrit, explains to her escort, or "intendit", as he is termed, what is taking place in the hall. She utters the non-IT word . . .

SAJUMMUL

But she reverts to her native IT tongue with the suggestion that they . . .

TAKKADEKKATIT

When Dauvit indicates that he does not wish to visit the bazaar she makes what appears to be two contradictory statements. First she requests him to cease grumbling . . .

STOAPMOANIN ABOOTIT

Then, with feminine fickleness, she invites him to resume complaining . . .

MOAN INTYIT

The damsel is, in fact, instructing him to accompany her into the hall. And there she points out to her intendit what she considers to be a modish article of male attire. The beauty of the IT language is heard in her enthusiastic call . . .

ERRARERRCHECKITJAICKIT-DAUVIT!

To this she appends the native word . . .

WHIRRABOOTIT?

He quickly ripostes with . . .

WHIRRABOOTWHIT?

With loving patience Margrit once more draws his attention to the checked garment. In so doing she breaks into a charming rhyme . . .

AWYURREALGLAIKIT
RANICECHECKITJAICKIT

She urges him to try on the jacket. But he demurs with an equally appealing stave . . .

ADREYTHERGONAKIT
THANWERRTHATDAMPTJAICKIT

But eventually he puts it on and his fair companion signifies her approbation with the lilting IT-word . . .

WHITTARERRFITDAUVIT!

At this juncture the lady in charge of the stall appears and after brisk financial negotiations she intimates to Dauvit in the IT tongue . . .

AFIFTIPEEBIT ANYIKINHUVVIT

But a grievous misunderstanding has

occurred. The checked jacket is not for sale. It belongs to a large gentleman who, feeling the heat, had placed it on the clothing stall while he had gone off to see a Mr James Riddell. Naturally he is considerably taken aback when he sees that a stranger is wearing it. He makes a stentorian protest . . .

DAMMITRATSMAJAICKIT! GIESIT!

He is further incensed when the lady in charge of the stall reveals her transaction . . .

ASELTIT

The large man then questions the lady's sanity and proposes that she should seek medical attention, advising her . . .

GETYURHEIDFELTIT

But now Margrit senses that danger is imminent and urges her lumbur to restore the jacket to its infuriated owner. Again the enchanting cadences of the IT language delights our ears as she warns . . .

AFFWITDAUVIT GIEITHIMAFOREYEGITBELTIT.

If I may use a word in that most difficult language . . .

GOADAHOPEYIZGERRIT.

The Professor joins

A Migration

From a reliable source I learned that, during the summer months, many Glaswegians forsake their native habitat and migrate to Spain. It is obvious to me that they do this in order to broaden their outlook and make themselves better acquainted with the life-style of those who are not fortunate enough to reside in the captivating city on the Clyde.

So I resolved to take part in the great international trek of these avid seekers after knowledge. I joined a band of these academic adventurers at the city's airport. You can imagine how impressed I was when I heard many of them using Spanish words and phrases. As we entered the aircraft one lady said excitedly to her husband . . .
AMFIERTO
AMFIERTO FLYINBOAB!

The gentleman commented with an affectionate . . .
AMIGO!
AMIGONNI HUVTI SUFFURRIS?

As the aircraft rose so also did the spirits of my fellow-passengers. One Spanish-speaking migrant looked down at the clouds which hung over his native city and remarked . . .
SIERRA

And he went on to explain to me . . .

SIERRA GLESCAFERRWERRA

It did my heart good to see the carefree camaraderie that prevailed as the flight to Spain continued. My fellow-travellers refreshed themselves with the traditional vacation potation . . .

JOOTIFREE

One celebrant held out his bottle to me with the warm invitation . . .

MAÑANA

quickly incorporating the Spanish word into his own language . . .

MANYANEEDAGIDDRAM

Great was the euphoria when we arrived at our destination. The warm Mediterranean air was filled with the joyous exclamations . . .

RATRIPWIZTOARTCHUR

JINGZAMJIGGURT

and

WHERZRALAVVI?

A buxom matron gave vent to her delight at being on Spanish soil with what I felt sure was an ancient Caledonian victory cry . . .

MABAHOOKISERRWISITTIN

But later I heard a lady express disapproval of the scaffolding that covered the walls of the half-built hotel into which she and her husband had been booked. Loudly she uttered the Spanish word . . .

ARRIBA!

She too adapted the word to her own native tongue as she informed her husband . . .

ARRIBAMPOATS SWINULTUS!

I was given to understand that she was referring to the travel agent who had arranged her holiday and that she intended to complain to someone. In fact she made skilful use of the Spanish for "to complain" . . .

QUEJARSE

She replaced the first syllable "QUEJ" with the sinister Glaswegian term . . .

KIKOANRA

But the great majority of the migrant Glaswegians pursued their sociological studies with the utmost assiduity, quickly becoming proficient in the local language. Outside a dress shop I heard one maiden declare . . .

RATPONCHO COSTA MINTAMUNNI

A pale-faced gentleman, after partaking of a seafood dinner, favoured the Catalan dialect . . .

OGOADMA KYTES GIENMIJIP!

And a lady whose husband, after visiting a bodega, lay on the sun-drenched beach, spoke of him in the local patois. She observed to a friend . . .

ESPANOL . . .

ESPANOL GITAZRIDZA BLIDDIFIRE

Ah, what gifted linguists are those intellectuals who make up the population of that glamorous metropolis in the West!

Rosemary

Helping the Bride

Rosemary, a somewhat domineering and at times tactless lady, speaks with a Glasgow suburban accent. In it the "e" and "y" sounds are usually rendered as "ai", as in "Mai, would you craidit thait!" and "a" becomes "e", as in "Fency thet, Elistair!"

Appropriately enough, Rosemary types are to be found in such naice raisidaintial districts of Glesgow as Milgai, Bearsdain, Whaitecraigs and Newton Mairns.

In this sketch we see Rosemary endeavouring to help her friend Ena whose daughter is about to be wed.

*   *   *   *

SCENE: The bride's bedroom.
CAST: ROSEMARY
                ENA
                CARRIE, the bride, Ena's daughter.

ROSEMARY: Is THIS where you are? Preparing the
                lemb for the slaughter! Your big day's
                come at lest, Cerrie! . . . You've been
                engaged quaite a long taime to Herry

	Berrie . . . Ena dear, you're not wearing THET het at the waidding, are you?
ENA:	Yes, I am. What's wrong with it?
ROSEMARY:	Nothing, nothing at all . . . Of course, Ai'm not med about flowery hets. They're all right on younger women, of course. Ai'd hate ainybody to say that AI was mutton dressed as lemb . . . Still, if you feel it suits you, Ena . . .
	ENA TUGS AT SKIRT OF BRIDE'S DRESS
BRIDE:	It's a bit tight, Mummie.
ROSEMARY:	Yes, it is . . . You know, Cerrie, since you hed thet holiday in Cennes with Herry lest summer you've put on quaite a bit of weight. Funny, isn't it? It's not as if you were an awfly big eater. (TURNS ASIDE AND SURREPTITIOUSLY COUNTS ON FINGERS) . . . Uh huh . . . You're a wee bittie pale, Cerrie. D'you not think a little make-up would help?
ENA:	She's got ON her make-up.
ROSEMARY:	Oh Ai didn't realaise . . . Better have another wee deb or two. It's always the same when one's going somewhere spaicial . . . One's gloves have shrunk, or one's hair's a mess or (PEERING INTO BRIDE'S FACE) . . . a spot appears on one's nose.
BRIDE:	(PUTTING HAND TO NOSE) OH!

ENA:	It's all right, Carrie.
ROSEMARY:	(TO BRIDE) Keep calm, dear. It's not a tairribly big spot. Ainyway, you can keep your veil down most of the time. (PICKS UP VEIL) . . . Is thet not the veil you wore at YOUR waidding, Ena? It's really quaite a good imitation of Bruges lace. Oh and you've menaged to get the brendy stains out of it . . . Ai still remaimber YOUR waidding, Ena, even though it was so many years ago. Ai thought you looked quaite naice in your waidding gown. It seemed to change your cherecter completely. You looked so sweet and innocent. In fect, Ai remarked on thet to the bridegroom's mother. "Whaite for purity," Ai said. "Whaite for purity?" said she, "There's hypocrisy for you!" . . . Maind you, she was inclined to be a wee bit TOO outspoken at taimes.
BRIDE:	(WAILS) Oh I wish it was all over!
ROSEMARY:	Now, now, cheer up, Cerrie. Remaimber, heppy is the braide the sun shaines on. (GLANCES OUT OF WINDOW). Mai goodness, would you craidit thet! It's raining like hell!
ENA:	Rosemary, would you like to go downstairs and keep Iain company?
ROSEMARY:	Och that husband of yours doesn't need ainy company! He's lying beck in the lounge with his feet on the coffee

	table and a huge whisky in his hand . . . He said something about being kissed bai a newt.
ENA:	Oh my God!
ROSEMARY:	What is it, Ena? Won't the belt go round her? (TO BRIDE) Make a big effort, dear, Trai to pull in your tummy.
BRIDE:	Mummie, did Daddy remember to book the photographer?
ENA:	Yes, yes, he's told Mr Flashman when to come.
ROSEMARY:	Mr Fleshmen? D'you mean thet wee photographer in the Haigh Street, the one with the paibble glesses? He took Brainda Spaindlove's waidding photographs . . . She wasn't awfly pleased with them. Mr Fleshmen made a little mistake.
ENA:	A little mistake?
ROSEMARY:	Yes . . . He shouldn't have toasted the bride BEFORE taking the photographs.
ENA:	What was wrong with them?
ROSEMARY:	Och it was just the engle they were taken from . . . Ai always think that people with prominent noses should never be photographed in profile . . . Cerrie, you insist on being taken full face only.
BRIDE:	(GRIMLY) Yes, I'll do that.
ROSEMARY:	Now don't look so glum, dear. In a week or two you'll be flaiying off on

	your Continental honeymoon.
ENA:	What do you mean, a week or two? They're flying off TONIGHT.
ROSEMARY:	Ai'm afraid not, Ena. Have you not heard? There's a strike bai air treffic controllers or something in Frence. All flights cencelled . . . Never maind, Cerrie, you'll get to Bidet-sur-Mer SOME taime!
BRIDE:	Who told you we were going to Bidet-sur-Mer?
ROSEMARY:	Oh, it was Deirdre Laidlow. Thet girl finds out everybody's grisly secrets! . . . Ainyway, we had a good laugh about it.
ENA:	What were you laughing about?
ROSEMARY:	Ai was telling Deirdre what happened to Elistair and Ai when we went to Bidet-sur-Mer. Of course, we should have known better. We went to the Hotel Splenderifero.
BRIDE:	WE've booked there!
ROSEMARY:	Ai know, dear. It's really a remarkable hotel. Each room with a view . . . of a brick wall. Elistair and Ai couldn't decide whether it was the food or the drains that smelled worse. Of course, you can always take air-fraishiners with you.
BRIDE:	(AGITATED) And . . . and what about the beach?
ROSEMARY:	Oh it's not all thet far away. After Elis-

	tair and Ai got over our wee bout of food-poisoning we braved the plague of wasps and mosquitoes and went down to the beach. Once you cross the motorway and the railway it's only half-an-hour's walk there.
ENA:	What's the sand like?
ROSEMARY:	Send? There's no send. Still, it's an interesting beach. Ai never saw such sharp paibbles. But there's a big sewage pipe that's hendy to sit on . . . (LOOKS AT HER WATCH) Oh but Ai cen't stend here all day gossiping! Ai'll have to desh home for mai fur coat. They tell me the heating system in the church is on the blink. Put on your laig-warmers, Cerrie. It'll be ebsolutely freezing in thet place! . . . Where are mai car keys? (RUMMAGES IN HER HANDBAG) Oh mai, Ai forgot! (PRODUCES TELEGRAM FROM HANDBAG) A telegram. It was on your hall table. Greetings for the heppy braide! Shall Ai open it for you?
BRIDE:	(DULLY) If you want to.
ROSEMARY:	(TAKES TELEGRAM FROM ENVELOPE) Yes, it's for you, Cerrie . . . (READS) "Cannot face it. Am going away". It's from "H. Berrie" Who's "H. Berrie"?
BRIDE:	It's from HIM! It's from Harry!
ENA:	Oh my God! The bridegroom's not

	turning up!
BRIDE:	I've been jilted!
ROSEMARY:	Keep calm, Cerrie . . . retain the cranium, Ena . . . You know, Ai never laiked thet young man. No manners at all. D'you know what he said to me? He said Ai was lecking in tect!

The Professor makes

A Gastronomic Discovery

A momentous discovery during my research into the Glaswegian language came when, on a visit to Paris, I entered a modest restaurant called Chez les Bachles. I found listed on its bill of fare a dish which bore the exotic title "Dumpline en Clûté Ecossaise". The portion I ordered was truly delicious and I requested that my compliments be conveyed to the chef.

Judge of my astonishment when the creator of the delectable dish proved to be a Scottish lady, the spouse of the establishment's proprietor. She addressed me in her native language . . .

"AWYIGOFUR RACLOOTIDUMPLIN?"

I begged her to let me have the recipe. With true Glaswegian graciousness she dictated to me the instructions on how to make that culinary masterpiece . . .

DUMPLINE EN CLÛTÉ ÉCOSSAISE

As long as ye keep the heid it's nae boather makin' a clootie dumplin'. First of a', gether thegither a ferr-sized basin, a big boul, a big poat, a plate that'll fit inty the poat, aboot a squerr yerd o' cotton cloath an' a dauda string. An' a kettle oan the bile.

Here's whit goes inty the dumplin' . . .

punna self-raisin' floour,
punna currants an' a haunfa o' raisins,
quartera punna suet,
haufa punna granulatit sugar,
fower wee teaspoonsfa o' mixed spice,
a big pincha saut,
some mulk.

Rummle up the hale jing-bang in the boul, addin' a wee tate mulk so's ye get a dough that's stiff an' no' runny. Tim some bilin' watter oot the kettle inty the fit o' the basin an' spread the cloath (or cloot) oan tap o' the watter.

Cowp the hale o' yur dough oot the boul an' oan tae the cloot in the basin. Draw the coarnurs o' the cloot the gither an' tie wi' the string.

Don't tie the string too tight or the dumplin' might burst efter swellin' up an' ye'll be in a helluva mess.

Noo ye've a big bag o' dough aboot the size o' a fitba'. Nixt ye pit a plate in the fit o' the big poat. Then gently ye lower the dumplin' oan tae the plate. Efter that poor as much bilin' watter inty the poat as will cover yur dumplin'.

Efter a' this cairry-oan ye'll mibbe waant a cuppa tea an' a fag or even a wee lie-doon. Anyway, whitivvur ye dae, don't let the dumplin' simmer fur mair than three-an'-a-hauf oors. Efter that time wheech it oot the poat an' oan tae a plate. Peel aff the cloot an' therr ye huv a dish fit tae set afore a dizzen Egon Thingmys.

Mr Ballhead as

The Ballet Dancer

Mr Ballhead is a character I've got myself into over the years on radio and television. He is a self-confident Glaswegian who holds forth with great eloquence to anyone who will listen to him. He enunciates carefully and has a fine Scottish contempt for English words and grammar.

In the following television interview he is seen in his role of Serge Jaickitoff, ballet dancer.

SCENE: A dance studio.
CAST: SERGE JAICKITOFF.
               MAISIE VISCOUNT, TELEVISION
               INTERVIEWER.

           *   *   *   *

               SERGE IS SEEN WHIRLING ROUND
               THE STUDIO, PROGRESSIVE
               FOUETTES INCREASING TO A
               VERY FAST RATE.
MAISIE: The man you are now watching is one
               of the world's most remarkable dan-
               cers. He is an incomparable artist, a

premier danseur of great renown, a man who has devoted his life to the ballet. He is . . . Serge Jaickitoff.

CLOSE-UP OF DANCER AT PRACTICE BAR.

SERGE: How are ye? . . . I was just having a small rummle-up before I get tore into Lez Silfyides this evening.

MAISIE: Mr Jaickitoff, I believe that, despite your name, you are of Scottish descent.

SERGE: (TAKING CIGARETTE STUB FROM BEHIND HIS EAR AND LIGHTING UP) That is correct. I made my descent on the world in the pretty little Renfrewshire village of Nitshill.

MAISIE: And the name . . . "Serge Jaickitoff"?

SERGE: Well, I may as well reveal to you that that is an assumed name, or nom dee dance, as we say. I decided for to use this cognomium after confabulations with my friend Nureyev. Him and I decided that Serge Jaickitoff sounded much more glamorouser than John Ballhead.

MAISIE: I see . . . You mentioned Nureyev.

SERGE: Yes. Ackchally he was the gent that discovered me. He was the first to realise that, as a ballet dancer, I was a natcheral.

MAISIE: How did that come about, Mr Jaickitoff?

SERGE:	Quite fortuatatiously. To let you understand, I was always noted for my louping propensities. I was what could be termed a congential louper. Of course, my farra assisted me to develop this unusual gift. Often he would give me what he called in his quaint Scottish way a scud on the gub. Consequentially I was louping from early infanticide right up to the age of adultery.
MAISIE:	And how did you come to meet Nureyev?
SERGE:	Eh? . . . Oh, big Rudy? Well, it happened in a very extraneous way. He was in Glasgow at tho time and he was walking along Great Western Road when, all of a sudden, he observed a most unusual sight. It was none urra than myself. I was in the act of louping on to the hin'-end of a scaffy wagon. That was then my vacation. "Bravo!" yelled Nureyev, "Bravo!" Then he came over and congratulated me. "Never," he said, "have I saw such perfect louping"! He talked impregnable English. Thereupon, without no further ado, we discussed my natcheral ineptitude for the ballet. Nureyev gave me the most unvaluable advice. "Huv a bash," he said. That very day I resigned from the cleansing department and soon I was on my way to

London to join the corpse.

MAISIE: What do you mean exactly . . . the corpse?

SERGE: The Corpse dee Ballet. Before you could say "Paddy Do" I became dedi-acatit to the terpsechorian art . . . Got a fag on ye? . . . Ta.

TAKES CIGARETTE FROM MAISIE, LIGHTS IT, INHALES DEEPLY AND COUGHS.

It must be the dust off that floor.

MAISIE: A male dancer, of course, must keep very fit.

SERGE: Aw, definately. To we exponuents of the ballet physical fitness is of para-noid importance. To let you under-stand, considerable feats of strength is called upon when we come in con-tract with certain ballerynas and other impedimentia of the ballet. For inst-ance, one has to be veriatable Col-osseum of strength when dancing with the celebratit Svetlana Bulginova.

MAISIE: Why is that?

SERGE: Well, you see, this large dansooze — often referred to as the Jumbo jet of the ballet world — is no lightweight. In addition, before she goes on the stage to embark on her balletical pererig-rinations she is very partial to a couple of pies with a pint or two of heavy. Hence, you can imagine that the burling round of this gargantuacious lady calls for more than a moducum of endeavour. Oh yes . . . Well do I remember setting her in motion during our performance of The Nutcracker Suit. So great was the velocity of those giant revolving haughs that I was propagatit across the stage with the most utmostest force. Before I could stop myself I hit the Sugar Plum Fairy a severe dunt right in the middle of her arabesque.

MAISIE: How unfortunate . . . I notice, Mr Jaickitoff, that you seem to smoke quite a lot. How many cigarettes do you smoke a day?

SERGE: Aw, not more than eighty . . . Mind you, sometimes I've got to borrow another twinty from big Svetlana.

MAISIE: I see . . . Well, I understand you're coming along to our studio here tomorrow for a recording of your new ballet, "La Tristesse d'un Petit Nyaff", which viewers will see in the evening.

SERGE: That is correct.

MAISIE: Good! We'll look forward to seeing you at 10.30 tomorrow morning.

SERGE: Oh hivvins, no' ten-thirty in the mornin'!

MAISIE: Why not?

SERGE: Ah don't stoap coughin' till two!

Mr Ballhead as

The Marathon Runner

Marathon running is one of Mr Ballhead's many activities. Interviewed on television by Maisie Viscount, he gives a modest account of how he achieved fame in that sport.

MAISIE: To John Ballhead the winning of marathons is one of the most important things in his busy life . . . Mr Ballhead, you are always running . . .

BALLHEAD: Aye, Ah'm always runnin' oota fags. Have ye got one on ye? (MAISIE GIVES HIM A CIGARETTE AND LIGHTS IT FOR HIM) Ta! . . . Aw, that's better. Nuthin' like a fag for gettin' yur braith back.

MAISIE: You are known as the Master of the Marathon.

BALLHEAD: That is so. Of course, my chinas call me "Shelfheid".

MAISIE: "Shelfheid"! That's a strange name!

BALLHEAD: Yes . . . Ackchally this unusual nom dee plum emanuates from the shape

	of my head. You may have noticed it sticks out at the back in no unseemly manner.
MAISIE:	Yes it does rather.
BALLHEAD:	Well, I may tell you that this stream-lined cranium of mines is at the foot of my success as a marathon runner.
MAISIE:	Oh, is it? Am I to take it that the specially light weight of your head gives you an advantage over other runners?
BALLHEAD:	No, no. It's a matter of airio dynamics. To let you understand — when I am running in a marathon the projecting portion of my skull cuts the wind resistance to a minewmum. Hence, at the rear of my napper a tempurry vackyum is created. Now the air rushes into this vackyum at such a dinger that my cranium is shoved forward with great acceleration . . . Of course, to keep up with it my feet have tae go like the ruddy clappers.
MAISIE:	That's remarkable . . . How did your running career start?
BALLHEAD:	Well, my proclivity for high-speed perambulating did not manifestate itself until I reached the age of indiscretion. It was then that I became deeply inflatulated with a young lady.
MAISIE:	Ah, she encouraged you in your ambition?
BALLHEAD:	She certingly did! The minute I sug-

	gested taking her into the woods to study nature she agreed. Without no further ado I grabbed her by the hand and we set off. Such was the velocity of my running that the young lady was rendered completely breathless.
MAISIE:	Weren't you breathless too?
BALLHEAD:	Yes . . . but not until we came out of the woods. Thereafter we made a number of high-speed visitations to these sylvan glades. Spurred on by love, I went faster and faster. I then became aware that I possessed this gargantuacious gift of running.
MAISIE:	I see . . . And how do you relax?
BALLHEAD:	Aw I usually indulge in jay-jogging.
MAISIE:	JAY-jogging?
BALLHEAD·	Precisely . . . Many a happy hour I spend amongst the traffic in Sauchiehall Street. You see, in many cities people are fined and otherwise inhibitated from enjoying themselves on busy thoroughfares. But Glasgow is more broader-minded towards pedestrians. As a result our freedom-loving city has became the Mecca for jay-joggers from all over the civilised world, and also from London.
MAISIE:	I didn't realise that.
BALLHEAD:	Oh yes . . . It may interest you to know that in 1985 Glasgow will be the venue for the Olympic Jay-Jogging Cham-

	pionships. I myself will be taking part in the two main events.
MAISIE:	Oh . . . and what are these events?
BALLHEAD:	Well, there's the 1500 metres Handicap Race in which the competitors jog across the street in front of two buses while perusing a copy of Playboy or some other instructive volume. Then there is the High Jump for the coveted Jay-Jogging Heidcase Cup. This simply entails getting out of a taxi on the wrong side and louping in front of a sports car driven by an inebriated short-sighted gent.
MAISIE:	It all sounds rather hazardous.
BALLHEAD:	Ah but you don't think of the dangers when your ambition is to be the Sebastian Coe of the jay-jogging world.
MAISIE:	I see . . . Well, thank you very much indeed, John Ballhead. I won't keep you any longer from your training.
BALLHEAD:	That's all right. I've already did my daily half-hour. I'm away home for a tightnur.
MAISIE:	A meal? Well, bon appetit!
BALLHEAD:	No, a HIGH tea . . . Is ma taxi there?
MAISIE:	You're taking a TAXI? But your home's only a 100 yards from here!
BALLHEAD:	I know, hen . . . But I hate walkin'. It tires me oot.

The Dog Called Parliamo Glasgow

It was to be the first time a Parliamo Glasgow sketch would be seen on an Edinburgh stage and Stanley feared the pantomime audiences at the King's Theatre wouldn't understand it. But they did and it wasn't a flop.

By way of celebrating Stanley dashed out to Corstorphine, bought a young pedigree boxer dog from a noted breeder there and gave it to me as a Christmas present. I wrapped the little animal in my overcoat and took him home to Glasgow by train.

Stanley suggested the boxer should be called "Parliamo Glasgow" and the pup was registered at the Kennel Club under that name.

Parli, as he came to be called, grew into a big powerful chap, a splendid specimen of his breed. He looked fierce but was the sweetest-natured of dogs and he was immensely popular with all who met him.

Appropriately enough, he quickly became au fait with various Glaswegianisms. Expressions that delighted him came from the young ladies serving in shops. His tail wagged in ecstasy when he heard . . .

AVABISKITFORPARLI

or

WANNAWEEBITLIVERPET?

'Parliamo Glasgow' or 'Parli' as he was known

But he seemed hurt when an anxious mother would bid her offspring . . .

KEEPAWAFAERATDUG!

with the quite unnecessary warning . . .

ITLTAKRAHAUNAFFYE!

But, reassured that Parli adored children, the mother would say admiringly . . .

ZANOFFINICEBIGDUG

or, proudly, . . .

RAWEANZNO FEARTFURRIM

All too frequently our canine heart-throb was offered titbits and great was his joy when he heard such questions as . . .

JIWAANTACHIPSON?

WULLAGIEMA WEEDAUDAMAPIE?

and

DIZZILIKESMARTIES?

Young suburban damsels seemed fascinated by his big brown eyes. He seemed to enjoy being fussed over by them as they gave vent to such eulogies as . . .

OHMAI HESGAWRJUSS!

and . . .

HEEZAREELLILAHVLIBOY!

A Kelvinside matron who visited us was surprised to see Parli sleeping back-to-back with the cat in front of the fire. He looked up perplexed when she cried out poetically . . .

FENCITHET!
BECKTOBECK
WITH YOUR
BIGBLECKCET!

Parli's popularity grew with the years and Glaswegian

generosity saw increased offers to him of steak, sole, pies, sweets, cakes, biscuits and even, on one occasion, a soupçon of smoked salmon.

My daughter, a dog expert, had a hard struggle keeping Parliamo Glasgow, the boxer, from becoming the fattest dog in Scotland.

Alex Mitchell

The Pedigree Certificate for 'Parliamo Glasgow' — a splendid specimen of his breed